ANSWERS FROM IMPROV TEACHERS

Book 2

DEDICATION

This is dedicated to the people who fail and try again.
To the people who fall and stand back up. To the people
who have a bad show, and get ready for the next one.

We're all cheering for you.

FOREWARD

Improv gives you the stage to challenge existing norms, call-out internal and external biases, tear-down oppressors and explore your curiosity. As an improviser, the onus is not just to play the best supporting role in empowering your fellow improvisers, but also holding this space of confidence within yourself. When you improvise on stage, your group is constantly trying to empower you and vice versa. You are then not only responsible for your group's upliftment, but in the process, responsible for your upliftment as well.

by Aarti Shastry

QUESTION

**"Do you have any tips on
how to enter the stage,
at the top of your set?"**

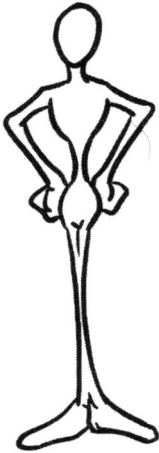

Emma Bird Enter with huge smiles at the audience and with each other. Make eye contact with each person in the team. Thank and praise the audience immediately for coming to see the show. Project 100% ease and confidence in your face and body. Look organised and comfortable in how and where you and the team are standing on stage.

Milou Manie I always try to go in very high energy, very bouncy, big smile, excited. I get nerves and this is very much a "fake it till you make it" approach. I am excited to be there, the nerves can just get in the way, so I exaggerate until we pass the initial "oh no, here we go" point.

Becky Webb Relaxed and alert are the two words I always try to focus on. Breathe and be present. You are there to perform to and for your audience not at them.

You are potentially introducing the greatest theatrical experience anyone has ever experienced, this set can be anything! Let that thought give you a shot of 'woo hoo' (technical term) and fire you out onto the stage.

Maggie Nolan Do: Enter on time. Be an ensemble. Look happy to be there.

Don't: Wander in late. Draw focus. Bring your bad day onto the stage.

Amey Goerlich Act like you want to be there and you are ready to entertain. Give off the energy you want back.

Shaun Landry As an actor? With purpose, enthusiasm and the mindset of "Tonight is the night of wonder."

Technically as an ensemble? I'm a huge fan of the "Reveal":

     -Introduction
     -Black Out
     -Music (with actors entering from the dark)
     -Lights up
     -Reveal of Joy

Just an extra added touch of theatrical polish :)

Chris Mead Do what YOU want to do. So many things in improv are done because we saw other teams doing them when we started watching shows. By all means, pile onto the stage to overloud, upbeat music and proceed to bounce off the walls for a few minutes, but only if that's genuinely how you want to start your show. Don't feel in any way like it's required of you. I've seen too many openings where the soundtrack screams FUN and the body language screams HELP ME, I WANT TO BE DOING ANYTHING BUT THIS. You don't want to come across like you're launching Windows 95 (https://www.youtube.com/watch?v=lAkuJXGldrM). Instead, think about your team, your form, your show and do something that honours and elevates that. Be intentional about the choices you make.

Kate McCabe Entering the stage STARTS with how you treat yourself that day. If you're performing in a show, try to get a good night's sleep before. Eat well during the day and generally take care of yourself. Once you get to the gig, do whatever warmup exercise energises and focuses you. Then, take a big cleansing breath, relax, and put your attention on your partner(s).

Charlie Gascoyne I always go in high energy, big smiles, and assume that everyone in the audience is as excited as I am. I want to set the right atmosphere of everyone feeling comfortable but also get everyone feeling ready to enjoy the hell out of an improv show.

Sarah McGillion I change some specifics for different types of shows. Always with shoulders back, head high, and aim to walk on to be close to downstage and right in front of the audience. Making eye contact with as many audience members as possible.

For a short form show, I go in with a huge smile, big energy, and depending on the crowd maybe running through and high five-ing and saying hello to the people at the back of the room.
For a genre long form show, I'll enter in the "mood" of the piece. In Noir, for example, walk on as an ultra-confident, stoic character.

Genki Kenny Energy without being too 'wacky'. Make the audience feel like you are excited to be there and you are going to give them the night of their lives. Connect with your team and make them feel like you are going to support them to give the performance of their lives.

Nikki Marie Morgan Energy is key for me, but I try to keep that energy focused, positive and engaging. I'll always be a big bag of nerves before a show so I think it's important to shape that into something that will work for me, my team and the audience. I may feel nervous, but I think it's important to channel that positively so your audience knows they're in safe hands.

Gosia Róża Różalska Enjoy it. Give them the first impression that you want to make. Are you a fireball? Are you smooth, are you cool, are you super happy to perform there, do you need a big breath, do you want to take the energy from music? They came to see you and listen to you. Don't panic, don't rush, do you. And connect to them, make them feel they are there with you, that you're reacting to them, even if you're not taking any suggestions, and that you're going on an adventure together.

Jane Morris Stand up straight. Smile at the audience. You are the host of the party you've invited these people to attend. They are about to play with you, those people out there. They are in discovery with you throughout the set. Include them.

7

I would appreciate it, as an audience member, if you didn't insult my intelligence by jumping around, or shaking yourself out like you're about to run a marathon. Do that on your own time.

Focus on the matter at hand. Which is a lot of fun.

QUESTION

"In rehearsals, I use silence and make big bold risks, but during a show I end up being more frantic and falling back on safe moves. How can I bring my rehearsal self into my show?"

Becky Webb Breathe. Always breathe. If you are feeling heightened, enter the stage on the out breath.

Emily Brady I am the most guilty of this! Whenever people ask me, I say I love to play grounded, emotional scenes, but 9/10 I'll end up playing completely off the wall characters in shows. One thing I found really helpful was to check in with my teammates before a show and say if we have anything we particularly would like to get out of the show. If I say I want a grounded scene, it's no small chance someone will remember that and guide my frantic self into one of those scenes. I think as improvisers we look after others first, so by signaling "I want to do this" you can give others the chance to help you get to it, and you can for them!

Kate McCabe *puts hand up* Yep. Me too.
But, I think a good way to look at this is to think about how you ground yourself in a scene.
How do you nail those feet to the floor and not run away from what is being built and from where your scene partner is going?

One exercise I learned from a great teacher was to try responding with what was JUST said to you before you respond.

11

For instance:

> Scene partner: *You said you were going to pick Carol up from Bingo, Linda!*

> You: *I said I was going to pick Carol up from Bingo....Dammit. I feel like I can't get anything right this week. Moving house has been tough on me.*

It gives you a second to digest what was JUST offered and make an honest reply to your partner. Not that having a crazy trip to the moon is always a bad thing. But sometimes we just want to connect.

Gosia Róża Różalska Keep practicing- feeling the audience is getting better with every show. And don't fall for filling-assumed-audience's-expectations. They came to see YOU, and what YOU want to tell them, and show them, they want to see that. A practical tip - if you start the show with a scene where you push yourself to risk and play this physical/silent way, the audience will take is as the exposition of the show, and "ok this is the show", and you will feel more confident and maybe you will not run away to your classical panic moves.

Sarah McGillion For me it is all about the level of trust and communication in the team. I can do long silent tension scenes when I trust that the team understands that there is nothing wrong, nothing to be "fixed." In practices and before shows we remind each other that silence is golden and those moments feel tense on purpose, there is no rush to find the "right thing".

Milou Manie Most my first performance experiences were also with my first troupe, and I learnt a lot of things between shows. Consciously thinking about one of those techniques before a show, maybe doing a specific warm up or just talking through that workshop again with the team allowed me to try one thing at a time. It does mean I haven't perfected any of the new things, but I've tried a lot of them.

Feeling safe with your team is the main importance here; I knew that 100% my team had my back, regardless if I tried something new or did "the usual." And of course I had theirs.

Genki Kenny I think nervousness, especially with a

new audience, or people I'm not used to playing with can cause me to go in too big sometimes. I think communication is key. If you are having this happen in every show then it is time to reflect on the reasons. I know I have sometimes been edited or talked over when I tried to be more authentic and grounded. Having played with different troupes, I realised that it was more about fear of being cut off than a lack of skill on my part. What is the troupe's approach? Do others feel the same way? A discussion about the rhythm of the show might be worthwhile to establish aims of each of the performers and the troupe as a whole.

Chris Mead A big audience response generates its own gravity. A single good laugh early on can actually pull an entire show off course. This is the root of the problem. In our nervousness we want to please the audience and laughter is the loudest response and therefore the easiest to identify. Frenetic, fast-paced performances are often the result of chasing those laughs. There's no quick fix. With experience we learn to trust ourselves more. I WANT to do grounded, emotionally connected scenes. I've SEEN the power in them. Laughter is a plosive response, a release. If we fall back on a well-worn schtick to get a quick laugh, we instantly deflate all the atmosphere we've built up. I just don't want to do that anymore. Craig Cackowski does this exercise where he limits lines of dialogue to 7 words or less. I've found that immensely helpful as a technique when I feel myself getting frantic.

Maggie Nolan Be honest with your team about your panic-moves and ask then to support you in avoiding them onstage.

Help each other in scenes. If one of your teammates is getting fast and frantic, play the opposite and be a snail. It will allow your scene partner to calm down and take a breath.

Charlie Gascoyne I've never even heard of emotional grounding, what's that???
Seriously, I think a lot of it comes down to nerves. Silence is powerful in improv but it can feel daunting and we worry the audience will switch off. So make your silence more interesting to watch: no- verbal skills, object work etc. Hold that pause and let it build, but don't switch off character completely.

Emma Bird Agree, I have this too. I think it's adrenaline, nerves, and excitement. What I try to do when I feel I'm doing this is to just stop talking. Really tune in to what my scene partner is doing or saying. It's like a part of me takes a step back or looks at the scene from a distance which enables me to reboot, slow down and offer something more grounded. Usually my next move then will be an emotional statement of how I'm feeling, or how I feel about my scene partner's character. Try to connect basically.

Shaun Landry By living less in fear of the unknown.

Make it a personal challenge

Or the simple improv adage: Dare to Fail.

QUESTION

"What are some characteristics of people you like to work with on improv teams? Not skills on stage, but what they're like to work with during rehearsals and in producing shows."

Milou Manie People who have drive and ambition, but aren't blinded by this. Passion is great, but can become an obstacle if it stops you from listening to people or sensing the mood, in a scene or in real life.

People who can share their passions rather than impose them can be incredibly inspiring. For me it's the difference between feeling "I have to do it their way" and "I want to do it their way!"

As a learner I know I have things to improve and am open to feedback, so working with experienced people who can tell me what didn't work, and how to improve that, are great. I've been lucky enough that almost all people I have worked with were great at giving feedback without making me feel like I'm no good at this.

And that's also the teammate and scene partner I strive to be: someone with ideas, but listening to others to then work towards the same goal.

And of course in general nice, kind people who respect each other. Perhaps I should've started with that.

Gosia Róża Różalska People, who are respectful to others. Who are curious. Who want to grow both as individual performers and as a group. Who want to participate in the creative process, instead of taking shows and festivals for granted without any work. Who are on time for rehearsals and warm-ups, even if we just talk about how we are for the first 15 minutes. Who share on social media, or somewhere where they feel comfortable, information about our shows to help the audience grow. Who look for new ideas, watch shows, and read books or articles and share with the rest of the troupe. And people who care about each other, and want to go on an adventure together.

Emma Bird People who are enthusiastic about the journey. People who are good listeners (in life). People who are active doers in running and administrating rehearsals and gigs. People who are genuinely happy to spend time with each other. People who are honest, kind, empathetic, positive and funny.

Nikki Marie Morgan I like to work with people who I feel care about the rest of the group. If we've discussed boundaries, you have listened and respected others' wishes, you'd be someone I'd like to engage with.

20

I love to have time to check in and catch up, but I also really value people who show up on time and commit to the rehearsal. Yes, I want to know if you've had a hard day and if that might be affecting you, but when a group has agreed to get together to work on a thing, I like to know that we're all committed to that goal.

Kate McCabe People who can observe what needs doing without me having to tell them...everything from 'hey, we need to warm-up before the show' to 'hey, these chairs need to be set up. For production and development of shows I also think communication is key: checking in with each other to see what we need to do next, what we can do better etc. People who have patience for the process...Optimists as well...but optimists who are tempered a bit by experience and reality!

Becky Webb People who understand that no one is bigger than the show. We are there to create this one thing for an audience. It doesn't belong to just one person. It is not a vehicle for ego, but an opportunity to create. Part of that is also the ability to critique and take critique. Not criticism. It is not personal but a chance to learn and observe from each other.

21

Part of that then, I guess, is trust. Trusting those who you are working with. Feeling as though you are in a safe space.

Shaun Landry People who are selflessly generous with a caring nature. Whip smart both in the idea of "book smart' and "street smart"
The same qualities of a life partner I wish for in a stage partner. Ironically enough? I produce and perform onstage with my life partner.
If I could produce, rehearse and perform with clones of R. Kevin Garcia Doyle, Betse Green, and The Obama's, I would. :)

Vanessa Anton I love seeing teammates who are really conscientious of each other and treat each other kindly. Who know how to talk through moments in scenes or shows that might have come up where everyone is not on the same page. I recently traveled with a team I coach for a festival and we shared a house and took on different roles in helping out. There was cooking and cleaning and family dinner together. One of the teammates asked everyone to share something they're vulnerable about. Over the weekend people opened up in their time and shared. One even did it later over messenger and acknowledged he hadn't been ready before. And they're various ages and backgrounds. It's really lovely to be a part of.

Genki Kenny I like to work with people who bring positive energy. People that care about you as a person as well as a performer, but support you to get out of your head for the good of the show and team. People who genuinely want to be there because they believe in the team / show and experience and share that joy of creativity. The most important thing though is someone who truly listens and uses that to connect.

Chris Mead I love improvisers who still love improv. Some people, there's a little disco ball embedded in their chest that throws glittering beams of light across the room because they are genuinely bowled over that they get to be a part of this brilliant art form. That's what I love. When someone is experienced and generous on stage and a total legend but they still giggle like a sugar-crazed toddler when they go on stage.

Charlie Gascoyne People who will listen. Listen on stage and in rehearsals, but also listen and reflect on things players say to them. I like to work with people who consider themselves learners.

Maggie Nolan I like to work with people that make that show or rehearsal a priority.

They attend practises regularly, keep show dates free in their calendar and engage fully when they attend.

If they aren't able to prioritise a team or show because life gets in the way, they take a step back for a while and let other people step up and get show time.

By the way, I am also basically speaking to myself with this answer, as I always over commit and then can't engage with everything properly. Like a damn fool.

Jane Morris I really only care about their skills onstage. But enthusiasm for a project is always a plus. People who can drop their crap at the door and work. And people who shoulder some of the responsibility of production.

Practice. Improvisation is a practice. The practice never ends. And frankly, it sounds like you don't trust the people on stage with you.

Catherine Hodges People who are genuinely good human beings and I would choose to hang out with. Supportive, fun humans!

QUESTION

"The coach of my improv team is pretty controlling. How do I best deal with controlling coaches or personalities?"

Shaun Landry This is long.

I got opinions on this.

I consider myself an actor who happens to improvise so I will refer to the term "Team" and "Coach" to "Ensemble" and "Director".

This is a very loaded question that leads to other questions:

> -Does the entire ensemble agree with the director of your ensemble on being too controlling?

> -Is it one person who feels the direction is too severe in control?

From those two spring up a plethora of other questions that boils into a big pot of "Oh my, this is not going to work out."

Is the idea of *dealing* or having *tactics* to work with a director actually toxic (This is my drama therapy talking. It's sort of tragic when it has to be applied to improvisational ensembles when I have usually applied it to humans who have been emotionally abused in a relationship.).

=====================

As an actor in an ensemble hiring a director:

29

-If the ensemble agrees the director is overly controlling, that director is not the right fit for the ensemble. Gracefully part ways and find a better fit in a director.

=================

If you are the only one who feels this and all/the majority of your ensemble does not feel that way...You can do two very simple things:

   - Listen to the note and do your best in the world to do that note.

   - you have the full right to say "this ensemble is not the right fit" and gracefully part ways.

====================

As an actor in an ensemble with a coach/director who hired you to perform:

   - know that you are a hired cast member and in the grand scheme of directing an ensemble the whole idea is their vision which also can be seen as control. Take the direction with grace and knowledge in the back of your mind that if you ever wish to direct, THIS will not be your method, but know you are stronger in knowing a particular person's way of directing an ensemble.

-Have a heart-to-heart with the director and have that conversation one on one for full transparency on how you are feeling. And if that does not work.

-Gracefully part ways.

====================

Storytime:

I have been performing for a very long time.

A very long time.

The very first ensemble I was in (a national ensemble that toured and we lived communally) was lead and directed by a man who was so incredibly volatile and verbally abusive (and yes. he got physically abusive too) that it was amazing the "Emotional and Deal Tactics" applied by ensemble members:

- Being a sounding board to the director when you do not agree with anything he does only bolstering the idea of bad control behavior.

- Having your head down and eyes low to hope to god to not be noticed while watching others be verbally abused by a controlling human being.

31

- And at 19...Others (like myself and a dear ensemble member I'm still friends with) would listen to music and drink. There was lots of drinking and music together. Lots of it. Then taking a drunken deep breath and dread rehearsal while continuing to do the work of someone who considered all of us "Stringless Puppets."

What happened? We left. Some stayed longer than others but ultimately it was an abusive company with an abusive director. He never fired a soul. We left. You can't always argue with a controlling personality. They don't view your quitting as a consequence of their actions. In their mind, you were not "Strong Enough" for "Good Direction. If you're at a breaking point, don't suffer for no reason. It's fine to leave.

==================

While these examples are around controlling personalities in the theater, they can apply to anyone dealing with this kind of person in everyday life.

Here's another resource:
https://www.goodtherapy.org/learn-about-therapy/issues/control-issues

This is good both for people who know they are

controlling as well as the people around them.

It makes me sad this question exists to where we have to go to therapy in improvisation...

When improv is usually promoted as therapy.

Know the root cause.

And respond to what you feel is best for the health of you and your ensemble.

...Gracefully.

Jennifer O'Sullivan Without more context this is a tough one to answer. Shaun's answer above covers many of the possibilities brilliantly. (Though I wish more people would say that Improv can be therapeutic but it is *not* therapy) . I would suggest also that there's a possibility of your and the coach's understanding of boundaries being a mis-match. What is the coach responsible for? What are you responsible for? Is anyone overstepping and encroaching on someone else's responsibilities, or is someone not taking care of their own so the other feels like they 'have' to step in? Talk through your expectations and assumptions with the coach and the team, approach it with curiosity not defensiveness, and find where the issue lies.

Jane Morris Leave. Get a new coach. Get real. You're not going to be able to control a controlling person.

Genki Kenny I'm a pretty non-confrontational person for various personal reasons, so I have found it difficult to make my opinions and voice heard in many situations both in work, acting and improv. For many years I was only working within one group of people and so didn't know any other approaches of coaching or teaching. At the end of the day, what do you want from the relationship? Is it serving you well and is that control supporting you to move on and develop as a performer? No? The very word 'controlling' is worrying. As a female performer, I have not been used to using my voice. More recently, due to finding support from other amazing improvisers I have been able to reflect and be more critical about projects that ultimately I am paying for. Many people start doing improv not to perform but to build confidence. A coach or teacher really needs to have some solid grounding in the skills of coaching / teaching in order to take care of the people they are directing or the consequences could have severe effects on the self-confidence of someone who is already struggling . If your improv experience does not make you happy then look elsewhere.

Chris Mead I think a good relationship with your coach is really important. If your coach isn't giving you what you need or seems to be on some sort of power trip then perhaps they're not the right coach for you? Dump 'em. Find somewhere who inspires you. I'm sorry if that sounds glib but we do improv to be enriched and delighted - if that's not happening then you owe it to yourself to find someone who you really connect with. And let's face it, there are a lot of coaches out there, they don't have to be more experienced than you - just willing to be an outside eye. And if the rest of the team is happy with the coaching ... perhaps it's you that's in the wrong team? Don't stay where you're not happy. Go and find the people that make your improv pinball machine flash all its lights at once.

Becky Webb Creative partnerships aren't a given because one person is a director and another a performer.

A partnership ultimately relies on what everyone is able to bring to get the best out of each and the work.

A stiletto is a classic shoe, able to create a wonderful silhouette, but I wouldn't play tennis in it.

It's ok to not click with a coach/director/outside eye.

35

It's ok to admit that the creative process is jarring and not working for you. But check in with it. For you, consider if the issue is their controlling behavior, or if you feel out of control and have a different vision to what you want the work to be. Are you taking feedback personally? Are you seeking validation from them? How does your group feel?

Likewise, assess if they are unable to facilitate a safe space to be vulnerable and creative, and if they are making the feedback personal. Are there egos flying around?

But, even if you are taking it personally, just be aware, accept that this is where you are right now in your process, and consider that you maybe need someone at the helm who can help steer you away from this tendency.

Also, just because someone is experienced, and has an amazing reputation, doesn't mean they will fit with you, and this doesn't mean you are wrong or a failure or a bad improviser. It also doesn't mean they are a bad coach.

Check to see if you are all on the same page creatively. If not, then consider if your coach isn't a fit for your group or if the group and coach isn't a fit for you. Either is no bad thing. It's important to enjoy it and feel as though creatively, you are getting out of it what you need.

QUESTION

"When you think of incredible improv performers, who do you know personally that you think just rocks the stage every time you see them?"

Kate McCabe I'm fortunate in that I know a lot of really inspiring improvisers.

My friends from Murder Inc and ComedySportz, Darryl Fishwick, Lukas Kirkby, and Jade Fearnley wow me every time we play together. They are absolute rocks you can depend on for a great show.

Carly Tarrett as well. One of my fave players because she commits to EVERYTHING whether it's mundane or way out in left field...she also makes hugely interesting choices and just has funny bones.

Jill Bernard, Erin Kennedy, Doug Nethercott, and MJ Marsh...all from Minnesota also rock my world.

Gosia Róża Różalska When I think of performers, who are always great to play with, I feel some things in common - they are ready to jump on stage with you at any moment, they take your offer and give it back with a surprise in it, they are joyful, having fun with you, and they make big choices, encouraging you to go bold.

41

Chris Mead Oh David, there are so many. I wouldn't know where to start. In this incredible international community of ours, I see brilliance at every turn. It's an embarrassment of riches. Sometimes I play a game in my head where I try to imagine the duo show I'd create with my favourite improv performers - what the format would be and what we'd call it. If I had to name people, it would be all the amazing artists I've actually got to perform those duo shows with. Katy Schutte (Project2), Lauren Shearing (Happy Accident), Emily Murphy (Unmade Theatre), Sally Hodgkiss (also Unmade Theatre) and Jules Munns (M&Ms). I'm also trying to persuade Gael Doorneweerd-Perry and Ella Galt to do duo shows with me so they absolutely deserve to be on the list too.

Maggie Nolan I really appreciate players that I play with rarely but due to their inimitable talent and generosity as an improviser, they make it very easy to connect with them onstage and create scenes and shows I am proud of.

Vanessa Anton, Liam Webber, Emily Brady, David Escobedo have all been incredible to perform with in the last 12 months even though we don't have a huge shared history.

Emma Bird I always am jaw droppingly impressed with Heather Urquart, Jen Rowe and Katy Schutte - all from the Maydays. They are incredibly funny, generous and playful - a little bit mischievous, which I really like.

Milou Manie I am lucky that here in Nottingham there are some fabulous people in MissImp that I adore watching and doing improv with. All those that regularly coach the weekly workshops or give the levelled course are great in sharing their knowledge and skills.

As I have Kate on Facebook and have spoken to her in person before I count that as knowing her personally, so I want to call out Kate Knight and Suzie Evans. When they performed as squidheart at a show organised in Nottingham I was simply enthralled, and felt like I had seen a new side to improv which was still funny, but also heart rendering and soft and quiet and loud and wacky and beautiful. I have since seen Kate in other performances and followed her workshops, but seeing squidheart again is very high on my list!

Jennifer O'Sullivan Christine Brooks. Utter commitment at every turn.

Jane Morris Dave Pasquesi. Susan Messing, Celeste Pechous, Jamie Moyer, Joe Liss. Jeff Michalski. TJ. Mitch Rouse. Jay Leggett (deceased now), Chris Farley, Danny Breen, Susan Messing, Dave Razwosky. The list is endless. Joel Murray. Ryan Stiles, Mary Wachtel, Ruth Rudnick, Ali Davis, Maureen Kelly, Rose Abdoo, Ian Gomez…I can't stop. Dan Castellaneta.

Charlie Gascoyne I couldn't name every single one because there are so many!! Ones who immediately spring to mind are Genki Kenny, Liam Webber, Ki Shah and Emily Brady❤

QUESTION

"I have a hard time when I compare myself to improv performers much better than me. What do you recommend when it comes to comparing my show to another team's show?"

Shaun Landry Shortest answer so far:
"Don't. Your show and you is unique on its own merit."

Charlie Gascoyne There's no one way to do improv and every performance is different: rather than compare, look at what worked for that troupe and let it inspire you.

Emily Brady The first time I ever saw the musical improv team ShowStopper! they did the most incredible show and I left the theatre feeling so depressed. I thought I'd never be able to get to that level, so what was the point in trying? I was doing a musical improv show in Edinburgh and considered myself to be good at it - then had my understanding of what "good" musical improv was] blown out of the water.

What I've learned since then is that "better" in improv is a very subjective term. Everyone has bad shows, and everyone has different styles! We're making stuff up out of nowhere - what does being "better" at that actually look like? Funnier? Cleverer? More considerate?

18-year-old me should have seen that show as something to aspire to and applaud rather than turn into a self-oriented carnival of doubt. My big tip - if someone makes you envious of their skill, try and sign up to one of their workshops or get them to coach your team! Learn from them! Do it!

Amey Goerlich It should motivate you to be just as good if not better. There will always be someone better than you and you will always be better than someone else. Celebrate good improv.

Emma Bird Try not to compare as it does nothing for your self-esteem. Instead, reframe it so you look at what they are doing that you love and take inspiration from it. Use it as an opportunity to learn and grow.

Vanessa Anton Give yourself the space to admire the others and wish to perform more like them. But don't let that overtake you. Always remember nobody else is like you or has that special thing you've got that makes your performance uniquely you. Try to find that balance between wanting to be better and appreciating yourself.

Gosia Róża Różalska First - think about what you admired and appreciated - it will show you what you find exciting, and maybe even only you paid attention to that, but it may show you in which direction you want to grow. And if you spot what was that brilliant thing, you can find ways to work on that particular skill. Because you don't want to be THEM. That would make no sense, because people make the best artists by being themselves, not copying someone else. But we can learn from other artists by finding in them a part of us that we want to improve. And if you see someone who's brilliant - just enjoy the ride and be thankful that you can still be amused!

Becky Webb The short answer is, don't. Just don't do it. The longer version is to first lose this terminology of "better than me;" it doesn't help and is not true. It may be that you are less experienced, still building confidence, and finding what makes you unique as a performer. To start using the term 'better' takes away from the variety that improv provides.
In terms of a show, this is it's own entity. Instead of comparing ask yourself, is

51

this show clear? Is the format how we want it to be? What do we want our audience to feel? How best can we do that? There are so many things within your show to be thinking about and continuingly developing.
Comparing creates a culture of judgement, particularly of oneself, and ultimately takes the focus away from your development.

Jennifer O'Sullivan Yonks ago I wrote a pair of blog posts about this. I reckon there's plenty there in this second half:

https://letstalkimprov.tumblr.com/post/7980732529 7/what-i-do

I think it would be good to offer a quick summary of the blog post here, for people who don't click through. Like: "If you're struggling, don't give up! There are so many resources that can help you to improve and still have fun." That's not a good example, but hopefully you see what I mean. It's such a short post you could consider including the entirety like with Chris below.

More thoughts...
You carry inside your memory a record of every single great and terrible show you have ever performed. You alone have an understanding of the heights and depths of the work you have made,

where you have struggled and where you have succeeded.

When you go and watch another show, you are only seeing a single, brief moment in the collective records of those performers.

How can you possibly compare your complete body of work to this one performance? Whether what you watched was good, or bad, or confusing - you don't know how they've struggled or succeeded in any other moments of their career.Take the show as a single data point, lean into what inspires you and leave the rest.

Chris Mead I also wrote a blog about this. Here's the text:

I'm scared to write this.

I've been thinking about it for months and I keep sitting down in front of the keyboard and suddenly finding a reason to do literally anything else.

Sometimes I get jealous of other improvisers.

There we are. I said it.

It feels like such an awful thing to say. Especially when our art form is all about support. We should be elevating each other's ideas, not shooting them down. Sometimes a show is so good, I pass through enjoyment and out the other side into jealousy. I start to feel sad. I compare what those brilliant improvisers do with my own paltry skills and I realise I haven't laughed for a good ten minutes. Instead I'm spiralling. My internal critic pops his squinty-eyed face around the doorframe of my subconscious and starts speaking directly to all my insecurities.

But I love improv so much.

One of the reasons it's so hard is because of my perceived place in my own improv community. I'm a teacher and a director and I play on a couple of teams that regularly tour internationally. I feel like I should be pretty good by now. I am pretty good a lot of the time. But every now and then, I can't stop myself from comparing.

Mark Twain said "comparison is the death of joy". Theodore Roosevelt said "comparison is the thief of joy."

But who said it better?

(bit of comparison humour for you there)

Either way, they're both right. You start comparing yourself to other people, your joy levels are going to take a hit. And unfortunately improv thrives on joy.

When I see an outstanding improv show — 95% of me is thrilled. Transported. Enraptured.

But that other 5% — oh boy.

I say all this for a couple of reasons. Firstly because if I feel like this, I'm sure other people do too. Hell, I KNOW other people do too. So if any of this chimes with you, know you're not alone.

That's important.

And secondly, I'm getting better. I've developed some strategies. And they work. So here are a couple of pointers for next time someone else's brilliance begins to tie your self-esteem in knots:

> - Tell people when they've had a good show. Don't sulk. Don't leave. Go up to them and tell them what you loved. Be specific. It almost always means the world to them. And doing something positive goes a long way to chase away the ambient negativity.

> - Understand that someone being amazing at improv, doesn't preclude you from being amazing too. This isn't a zero-sum game. The world is wide enough for Hamilton and me, as Aaron Burr once memorably sang. I know this seems simple but REALLY try to

55

internalise this idea. Improv prowess is not a finite resource.

- Finally, remember that improv is first and foremost an art form but it's also an incredible community to socialise within. Watching people be goddamn insanely talented is the natural consequence of knowing a load of goddamn insanely talented people. It goes with the territory. Enjoy it. Look who you get to be friends with.

I feel much better about this stuff nowadays. I feel like I've claimed back a part of myself — that bit that fell in love with improv in the first place.

My final 5%.

And I know I'll never sing like Rhiannon or play characters like Cariad or think as quickly as Katy but that's alright. There are other things I can do better than them.

Like jump chairs.

Even better, we get to use all that talent to make each other look good.

And that makes me feel joyful all over again.

Jane Morris Comparison is the thief of joy. Ask your therapist about your self-esteem issues. Leave them at the door of the theater.

Kate McCabe Hmmmm...it's a gift and a curse, isn't it? Comparison.

Being knocked back by the skills of another troupe doesn't mean that your show isn't good. So, first, accept that and feel happy about it.

Second, rather than feel diminished, try to feel inspired by this. If a show 'wows' you, have a think about what it was that they did that impressed you so much? Be moved to work towards the qualities that you strive to be.

To paraphrase a more popular life philosophy...be the improv you wish to see in the world.

QUESTION

"I sometimes feel fake promoting myself or my shows. How do I get comfortable promoting myself? Is it important to promote myself?"

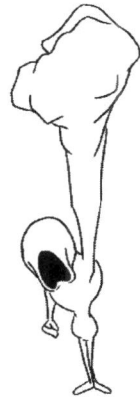

Amey Goerlich It's all part of this business of entertainment. Usually it's not just promoting yourself but also your team, your theatre. I'm thankful that I don't have to pass out postcards in the middle of time square anymore to promote shows. Social media makes it so much easier and you can get creative with it. Buckle up because you will forever have to promote yourself in this field, even when you are huge.

Gosia Róża Różalska Oh, depending on where you're from the answers may be different. I can speak for myself - for me, as a Polish person who was told "not to brag", and "be humble" from everyone since being a kid, it's very uncomfortable. Because of my work, a few years ago I decided to make a fanpage on Facebook, and this feeling still hurts, because "who am I...".

My personal advice would be - if you don't promote your show, people will not know about it, and they won't come even if they wanted. If you're scared you will annoy people - they may just stop observing you. If you're scared people will judge you - they will, they always do. On the other hand, don't go crazy with posting the same thing over and over again, because even interested people will get tired if that. And please, this is really my thing, I know, but when you send invitations on social media, and your show is in a city A, don't send that to everyone, who live in city G, X and Z 800km away, or in a country 3000km away. It makes people like me just block future invitations from you. Spend ten minutes more to choose people who may actually come to this show.

Louise Woods Yeah, it's part of the job. Actors have to do press to promote movies. Different mediums and scale but same thing.

Shaun Landry Long answer: you are doing theater to the wind if you do not promote your shows, your ensemble or yourself. If you feel uncomfortable/not good doing so I recommend finding a person who will.

It's a skill to make a press release talking in the third person. And it's only fake when you outrageously lie about it. It's a skill and a necessity every actor should have.

Short answer: Shaun Landry thinks it's important. Check out her website at www.shaunlandry.com

Milou Manie If you feel you can't promote yourself, pretend it's your friend who is performing - what would you do to help them get audiences to their shows? Then do it. You're worth it just like anyone else!

Unless you tell people, how should they know about you? Having an online presence can help, though of course only if you are able to maintain that; better to have one active social medium than a zillion with no updates. Network. Get a small local paper to review you. Ask venues where you perform to promote your show on their own channels. It's a lot of hard work, but over time you will be able to build relationships, prove yourself, create a fanbase, all of which should help spread the word.

Emma Bird promotion is just part of being an entertainer or teacher. If you don't promote, how will people know or access what you're offering? I frame it as information awareness not an ego thing. I want people to access improv because improv is ace, so telling people about how and where to access it is part of information dissemination. If no-one comes to your show or class, then what's the point? I want people to be entertained so they can enjoy laughter, I want people to learn improv so they can potentially benefit from that experience.

Jennifer O'Sullivan In terms of promoting shows, think about the promise you are making to your audience. What are you hoping they'll feel, experience, enjoy? Share that with them in all of your communications: social media, emails, event listings, posters, etc etc. The way they engage with your show starts way before they take their seats.

And if you feel weird promoting it, ask yourself 'why did I make this show? Why do I want to share it? Why should anyone watch it?'. Those are your reasons for promoting it, and it is perfectly acceptable to want to share your art - especially one that is so dependent on an audience!

Chris Mead Nah. It's part of the job. You shouldn't feel bad about promoting yourself. If you're proud of the show, write about why and ask people to come and see it. No problem there. It's still their decision.

QUESTION

**"What are so good habits to
get into if you want to make a good
impression on
your improv teacher?"**

Shaun Landry Do the work, take risk, dare to fail. Ask questions.

Becky Webb I would say good habits and impressing your teacher a two separate things.

Good habits are about making it about the work, connecting with your class, leaving your outside stuff at the door, and respecting yourself and your classmates.

Trying to make a good impression contradicts this as you are making it about you and concerning yourself with how you are being perceived. Be present with yourself and the room. You're enough.

Emma Bird Be committed. Be enthusiastic. Be supportive of others in and out of scenes, especially new people who attend a workshop for the very first time. Enjoy everything with the spirit of YES. Let your teacher know you appreciate them, their skills and support.

Vanessa Anton Have kindness and respect for your classmates. Look out for each other and be patient. I don't care how talented someone is, kindness makes me believe in someone's work. Be good to each other.

Amey Goerlich Take the note then implement them in your scenes. Show respect and don't talk over them. Be there to learn, not to judge the process. Lift others up in class and play with the people others won't play with.

Louise Woods Listen. It's an important skill both on and off stage. Listening while having a growth mindset and being open can change your life.

Milou Manie Be willing to get feedback. I am still scared of being critiqued, but there's nothing quite like a bit of sidecoaching that really helps me understand what I am doing, and how I can elevate myself, the scene, and/or my scene partner.

Learning to me is about respect for someone else's knowledge and their willingness to share that. The same goes for your fellow participants: respect that they are also trying to learn, so don't hog the teacher, but also don't take learning possibilities away from someone else.
I suppose the above is not really about impressing the teacher, but I don't think impressing anyone should be part of going to a workshop or a course. he reason for going is internal transformation, not external validation.

Chris Mead Buy your improv teacher gifts like the latest iPhone or some really high end chocolate. I like anything with over 70% cocoa solids. Single origin preferred.

(real talk: you shouldn't be trying to impress your teacher, you should be supporting your classmates and making them look good in every scene you're in with them.)

Jennifer O'Sullivan Remember that they may be teaching you exercises and techniques you already know, but with a different focus. Pay attention to your own work, and don't backseat teach (offer notes to other students etc). Ask questions when you need clarification, but try not to derail. Take care of yourself - you know your personal limits and boundaries and it is very okay to hold onto them. Let them challenge your creative safety, not your personal safety.

Amey Goerlich Take the note well and execute it in the very next scene. Show you are here for it and only want to get better. Respect your teacher's input, and work hard even if it's slow.

Emily Brady I would say don't worry too much about impressing your teacher. If you are too obsessed with being "the best" in a class or rehearsal, you're in your own head and limiting your own learning.

QUESTION

"I have a hard time remembering names and where people put the object work table ... how can I help remember all the details for a show?"

Catherine Hodges For remembering names and details, one warm up my group plays is a pattern game, bestowing one person in the circle with a name and some characteristics. That person then bestows a name and characteristics onto the next person, then the next, then the next, until everyone is a unique character and we've built a world. And then we go round the circle and try and remember everyone and their relationships, and as we practice and get better at the game, we make these details increasingly complex to train ourselves to remember (and also build interesting worlds/relationships/characters).

In an actual show when I can't do this, or when I need to remember space work, I like to set words or steps or actions to an imaginary beat - drumming the names into my head, but also then it helps me to remember the bar is three beats away from me and I can run my hand along it for two beats in length.

Jennifer O'Sullivan As well as all the advice for practicing: Trust your fellow players will help you out without making you look foolish. (Aka, fellow players: don't correct them in a big 'OH HEY LOOK AT YOUR MISTAKE' kind of way. Can you accept their offers of new names or changing room space and make the forgetful person look good?).

Becky Webb For me, the main thing is to focus on being relaxed and alert. If you are focused on how you can't remember then you won't, because you won't be present.

Keep practising. In rehearsal use games where you physically map out an area, or define a location and your colleagues have to guess can get you thinking about being in your body. Improv isn't just the voice.

A trick I sometimes use is to give someone their name. "correct Dave, it's the triangle..." as it's come from you, you are more likely to remember.

Chris Mead Important question: are you not remembering that stuff or are you not even noticing it in the first place? Because those are two different problems with two different solutions. If you're not even noticing the things going on in your own show then may I humbly suggest that you go back to improv fundamentals and PAY ATTENTION? Do your scene partners the honour of being present on stage. Listen even if you're not in the scene. If the problem isn't attention then it's being intentional about remembering - repeat character names in your head after they're introduced, really notice the outline of the objects being delineated. These skills are improv muscles and like any muscle you want to improve, you need to isolate them and get in the reps. (I mean, I've heard, I don't really know how gyms work) PRO TIP: you don't even have to be in the show to stretch these muscles, you can get in your practice by watching other people play.

Emma Bird I try to be hyper alert to names and objects. So I'm actively observing and clocking these touchstones as they are named or as they appear in a scene. If it's names I'm hearing, I repeat them in my head immediately a few times, then I actively vocalise their names as soon as I have the opportunity. If it's objects, I observe where they are, make a mental note, and try to use or touch them as soon as I have the opportunity.

Kate McCabe One simple thing you can do is use the things as they get established. That can include names and objects/ environments. Make the connection as tangible for yourself as you can.

Jane Morris Whatever. Does the audience really care that much that the refrigerator door handle was a foot off? Can you keep track of what's really happening in the scene? That's way more important.

QUESTION

"What is the difference between an intermediate and advanced improv performer?"

Emily Brady 10% experience, 90% the confidence to call yourself "advanced."

Sarah McGillion Understanding that a show is a show. Good shows come and go and you cannot live by your last "best" show, nor can you become highly distressed when you have a bad one. All are learning experiences.

Chris Mead When you get to the point where you're not worried whether you're an intermediate or advanced improv performer ;)

Jane Morris I've never much believed in stratifying players. Paul Sills said, "whoever comes, plays." If I had to answer this I'd say, "can the players tackle creating a new form?" That would be a good indicator. Another would be, "Does the player take direction?"

Emma Bird I've been thinking about this question a lot.... For me, I think that when I watch advanced players perform, what makes them different from intermediate is how seamless the mechanics of improv are stitched into their 'way of being' on stage. I've watched some exceptional performers, and I'm sitting there and I can't figure out how they're doing what they're doing... and I'm really trying to see the mechanics and structures (because that's the way my brain works), I'm quite analytical when I watch theatre or improv. And oftentimes if I'm watching advanced performers, I soon give up on trying to analyse and identify the mechanics (what 'form' is this? What structures? What skills and techniques am I seeing?), because those elements are so embedded in their practice; they are minute stitches in the fabric of what they are doing. And they have often been doing improv for decades. (I'm thinking about The Maydays, and the smash teacher team at Copenhagen Fest 2019 of Jaime Moyer, Jay Sukow, Craig Cakowski, Brian Palermo. I literally sat there watching their nightly shows with my jaw on the floor!).

Becky Webb A certificate framed on your wall!

I get the practical sense of it, but I actually don't know how valuable it is to quantify it in such a way. It suggests the idea of being ahead, or above others and gives a competitive nature to how you view others you are working with.

You may have more experience performing to an audience, have taken workshops with a variety of teachers, and have been doing it for years. But if you think you have no more to learn or don't need to go back to basics at any point, then you are doing yourself and your colleagues a disservice.

Isn't one of the best things about improv the fact that there is always something new?

QUESTION

"I hear all the time to 'connect to my scene partner.' But what does that really mean? Is it just eye contact and listening?"

Shaun Landry We connect to our scene partner the same way we connect to a human offstage whether friend or foe.

We as actors bring that to the stage in heightened form.

We listen to our scene partners and the gifts they create in that moment. We respond to our scene partners. We express how our characters onstage feels towards each other

Connecting to someone in this world off the stage is exactly what it has always been. Showing emotion. Listening. Eye contact. Reacting and responding. Having a point of view to what is said onstage.

We create the world around us.

We should do this onstage, but heightened.
It is the same technique applied to classic theater.
Look someone in the eyes and say what you are saying like you mean it.

And sometimes all it takes is to look into a person's eyes in character, just like offstage when you tell someone you are hurt or you love them

Just like offstage, when you tell someone you are hurt or you love them.

Catherine Hodges For me, connection to another person is about opening up myself to be vulnerable and trust my partner enough to really listen and connect with what they say, and display my honest (albeit sometimes heightened) emotional reactions to their actions. But it's less about a physical thing to do with the other person (e.g. eye contact) and more an internal emotional state to be able to put trust in my scene partner and say how my character actually feels in regards to their actions.

Charlie Gascoyne For me as a performer, eye contact isn't something I can establish easily, and I know for many neurodiverse performers that I have worked with, it's the same issue. But connection can come from so much more; don't just listen and respond to what is said, think about how the character is FEELING. Look for other non-verbal clues like tone, facial expression, context etc. Tune into their wants, their goal, their motivation and think about whether your character is aligned to their cause or against it. If you aim to get a full and comprehensive 'feel' for your scene partner, you can begin to move forward in the scene with a sense of 'togetherness.'

Emma Bird I agree with all the above too. I think connecting might start with looking at someone's eyes. But for me there's always an internal mindset or a 'heart-set' of warmth and kindness towards a scene partner. I set my heart and mind towards them with openness, willingness to support and listen, I try to radiate an energy of acceptance, kindness and fun toward them. That's me as a person, connecting with you as a person. What my character does may be different- I could be a grumpy character in that particular scene or moment, but that's not where I'm at as a human/actor/improviser, that's what I've chosen as a character.

Kate McCabe Eye contact is terrific as is anything that helps ground the two of you... but beyond that important connection, consider what your scene partner wants throughout the scene. Be what they need. That doesn't mean, necessarily, that you heed their character's commands (know the difference between the character's wants and the actor's wants). The character might say 'don't go!' But as an actor and scene partner you can see what they want is for you to storm out. Connect that way. Honour them by playing how they want to play. Enjoy the push and pull with them. Connect by playing together and learning to 'read' their needs. The more you play with someone the more you'll be able to connect.

Jennifer O'Sullivan Be curious and care. Think: 'It matters to me what this person says and does'. If you care about them, you've built half of the connection, and it'll be easier for them to meet you with their half.

Chris Mead I could talk about this forever. I'm obsessed with the idea of connection in improv. I'm constantly tinkering with the specifics but currently I think it boils down to this.
Make eye contact. Feel something for your partner. Listen and allow yourself to be changed. Make ONE offer at a time. Use specifics. Seek connection - emotional, mental, physical. Look for enthusiastic consent. Assume knowledge and seek intimacy. Be vulnerable, share something authentic. Rejoice in silence. Notice everything. Make everything important. Laugh. Play. Take risks. Get into trouble. Fall in love.

I think that about covers it.

Becky Webb For me it is about connection and creating a shared experience. Whether it is to an audience - either on stage, the street, a one to one - or when meeting new people in everyday life. The tools and ideas that improvisation gives you are so valuable in helping to create that.

Ultimately, we only ever really have the present. So, let's see where that can take us.

Jane Morris "Connecting to your partner" is what it means to improvise. It's not a 'thing" you do. It's all you do. It's where the scene lies, in the space between you. Just like music is not the notes (that's the tune) it's the space between the notes. Connect physically. Move when they move. Move because they move. Reference their movement. You don't have to know why. Your body will inform your mind.

Follow the follower. All you have to create the scene is what was just said to you, or what just happened.

When in doubt, do one of two things. Read the demeanor on the face of the other player. Whenever you are lost, read. "You look shocked." "You are tired." This not only tells the other player what you are seeing (what you really see, not what you want to see to jigger the scene or advance your agenda), it tells the other player what the entire audience is seeing. Plus, it kicks open the door for the player to respond with an honest response.

And/or: just say this, "So what you're saying is…."

And repeat what your partner just said in your own words. Now you've gotten beyond 'story' and into 'idea'. And now you can play.

Maggie Nolan Eye contact is a great start, but I like to demonstrate my relationship with them as quickly as possible. So, building a warm smile between us, eyeballing them with a disappointed sigh or hovering nervously around them... whatever it is to let the audience know there IS something there between us and therefore draw them in and get invested.

QUESTION

"There is the 'Johnstone Camp' and the 'Del Close Camp' and the 'Spolin Camp' and more...why do these camps spring up? And why do we view them as in opposition to each other?"

Emma Bird I think they're just part of the evolution of the art form. These theatre makers were trailblazers and evolved their various schools of thought over time. Then they trained people up and inspired performers and actors to continue. And they grew. It took me a while as a beginner to get my head around the idea that there were different iterations of improv. And I think each of them offer creative possibilities for all improvisers. And I guess some performers grew to prefer some over others. But I think there's cross pollination between them and each has huge value to the art form as it continues to evolve.

Kate McCabe I think it's in our human nature to want to form tribes. We do it all the time and we see it in religion, politics, sports, and even rival comic book companies! It's no wonder that it happens in something as personal and emotional as improv.

The good side of this instinct is that we grow communities and feel like part of something bigger. The downside is the stubbornness of feeling 'right' in comparison to those who think differently than you do. It can lead us to allow our more vitriolic sides to take charge.

Overall, I think it's wise to learn to appreciate the wisdom and insight of many influences. No one person or teacher contains all that there is to know.

Being welcome in many tribes is better than stagnating in the one.

Chris Mead As long as we've had human society, we've felt the need to break social groups down into the 'we' and the 'not we'. There are very good evolutionary reasons to do this. It's helpful to have a tribe, especially when the stakes are life and death. And it's hard to break the habit - though improv is hardly facing down sabre-toothed tigers with a sharpened stick (except when it is). Defining a school of thought helps you define your terms and creates something teachable. Partisanship is a natural consequence of that. But really it's just a matter of vocabulary. We're all doing the same thing in the end. I'm not sure I see the long-term benefit of putting ourselves in little boxes and affixing carefully-worded labels. In my experience, the very best of us, whether Johnstonians, iO faithful or UCB die-hards, can play together just fine. They've all come to the same conclusions, though the routes they've taken are very different. For my part, I want to take all the classes, learn from everyone and synthesise something that's uniquely me from it all. Steal like an artist, as Austin Kleon says.

Jane Morris Because no one teaches the history of these "camps". Viola Spolin invented what we do. I'm shocked and amazed by how few people know that. Her son Paul Sills furthered that work and founded the Compass Players and the Second City. Del Close took that same work (along with other people) to night clubs, where the play had to be faster and the "games" were codified by that company (which was located in St. Louis.) He later worked with the Committee, which is where The Harold was born, but not in the form we now use. He codified that after his years as a SC director. That is the direct lineage.

But now those people aren't here anymore to explain what they mean when they said whatever they said. So, now it's like the Bible. There are people who really do understand it and what it all meant. And there are people who find one phrase that they get stuck on and it's their whole curriculum. And yes, I personally have a lot of opposition to that.

I will give you another answer that is as cynical as it is true. You are taking classes from people who want you to take classes from them. They have figured out what a cash cow you are and so they add level after level to a tiered program that actually has no prize for you at the end. They need to brainwash you into thinking their way is not only the best way, but the only way. Hence, camps.

QUESTION

"Why does improv still interest you after all this time?"

Emma Bird I'm interested in the intersection between well-being and participating in improv. I see it all the time at my classes. And it is lovely! I also see people discovering their playfulness and creativity once again, and without judgment. I enjoy seeing people supporting one another's creativity and imaginations. I love seeing people validating other people and being supportive and kind. I love hearing all the laughter week in week out. And I love laughing myself, every time I teach. I am lucky to have a job where laughter is inherent and abundant. I also am still challenged by it personally, still growing, learning, developing my own creativity and play. I love the craft of it, the boundless skillset, and it's still exciting to watch, perform and teach.

Chris Mead If you're creative (and I think all human beings are creative at something) then part of the spark of that creativity is an insatiable drive to get better at the thing you love. Improv is a maze of possibilities. It's a skill tree of vast and multi-faceted complexity. I can't imagine ever getting bored, of not having something new to learn. And the more you perform and teach and take classes, the more avenues open up. I'll be 129 years old and mostly machine parts and I know I'll still get a kick out of learning a new warm-up. Add to that the fact that improv skills have actual applications in everyday life and I can't see me ever losing interest.
Becky Webb For me it is about connection and

creating a shared experience. Whether it is to an audience - either on stage, the street, a one to one - or when meeting new people in everyday life. The tools and ideas that improvisation gives you are so valuable in helping to create that.

Ultimately, we only ever really have the right now. So let's see where that can take us.

Jane Morris Engagement with the other players and the audience keeps me interested. Here is something Del Close said that is the key to that excitement, the reason it all seems like magic. "When the first player speaks, the possibility of response by the other player is infinite." The audience is at least subliminally aware of this. Comedy really is only two things: Recognition and surprise. So when we all find out what's happening, what the scene is about, where the players are, who they are to each other…none of us know that as the scene begins. When we discover it, we discover it together, audience and players. We land at the same time. That's the magic. Stay in discovery, don't write, or plan, or do anything but follow the follower, and you're there.

Amey Goerlich Seeing people discover the beauty of improv and building a scene with others is truly magical.

BIOGRAPHIES

Vanessa Anton

Vanessa Anton teaches and performs in San Diego and wherever else anybody will let her. She loves to travel, go on improv adventures, and make new friends all over the world. She is in constant search of a better world through improv.

Working with vulnerability in improv is her favorite aspect of the craft. She enjoys helping students and performers find honesty in the things they often dislike about themselves and find better connections to each other.

She has taught her vulnerable workshop in San Diego, Phoenix, Orange County, New Hampshire, and Nottingham, UK for Improv Fest Ireland and Camp Improv Utopia.

Vanessa is currently the Director of Vulnerability and Inclusion for Cornerstone Improv in San Diego, and enjoys the team and community.

113

She loves to dance like a dork and pet all of your dogs. She has worked in human resources for over a decade. She is also enthusiastic about yoga and music. And she hopes to meet you, if she hasn't already.

Emma Bird

Emma is a professional actor, director and improviser. Some highlights include The Royal National Theatre with Frances de la Tour, a regular character in the TV series Casualty, the feature film "The Governess" with Minnie Driver, and the screenplay "Needle" by Jimmy McGovern with Pete Postlethwaite.

Emma has directed award-winning theatre at Brighton, Liverpool, and Manchester Fringe Festivals.

She trained in improv by The Maydays in 2007, with further training from world-class teachers from iO, Annoyance, and Second City.

Emma founded Liverpool Comedy Improv in 2015, teaching and performing improv in the North West UK. She has co-founded three improv teams, The Hee Ha's, and The Unscriptables, and Boss Birds. For more info see:

www.liverpoolcomedyimprov.co.uk

Emily Brady

(Photo by: Sam Staniforth at IsoElegant Photography)

Emily is an instructor at MissImp in Nottingham, and is on the production team for the Robin Hood Improv Festival. She performs on numerous teams such as Rhymes Against Humanity, It's a Trap!: Star Wars Improv, Mind MELD and more.

Emily also produces and hosts the Improv Treehouse which interviews improv teams all over the world! It's a great library of the improv community and what drives them.

Monica Gaga

As seen, heard and staged on BBC3, London Live, BBC History, BBC Radio London, Global Pillage, The Comedy Store, Hoopla Impro, Boulevard Theatre and more...

Monica Gaga is a British-born black African queer improviser, facilitator, host and scripted actor and performer.

She trained in Community Theatre at East 15 Acting School, and her boundless love for improv stems from time spent at Second City in Chicago.

When she is not performing, hosting or teaching, Monica is championing diversity in improv and trying to get as many people, particularly POC, involved as possible.

Monica is based in London, UK.

Charlie Gascoyne

Charlie is an improviser and performer from Sheffield, making up one half of Little Chicago Comedy Productions, and one half of gruesome twosome Long Boi and The Noise. She's a big fan of character work, bold choices, and surreal weird improv. She cannot do accents. She can barely do her own accent.

She's performed at Edinburgh Fringe, award-nominated at Leicester Comedy Festival, improvised on BBC radio and was twice crowned Improv Smackdown Champion (a very very serious improv competition...honest!).

When she's not on stage she's training to be a Speech Therapist, often combining improv and speech therapy to teach workshops on communication.

Amey Goerlich

Amey is the only female in the 18 year-old UCB indie quartet known as KROMPF. She teaches her KROMPF classes independently in NYC & in LA. She has taught her game workshop at many improv festivals around the country including The Tampa Bay Improv Festival, The Torch Theatre, The Pocket Theatre, Omaha Improv festival, San Diego Improv Festival 2017, Improv Utopia East and West and more.

Currently she lives in Los Angeles, teaching and performing at M.I.'s Westside Comedy Theatre. She also runs The Improvisation Training Hub for independent Improv teachers in NYC & LA. She co-created an improv card game called 'Humans Being an Improv Card Game' available on amazon.com.

She hosted and Coordinated Indie Cage Match at UCBeast for 5 years 2011-2016. She was the Artistic Director of the virtual theatre E-MPROV. A long form improviser from 2001-2016 at The Upright Citizens Brigade Theatre in NYC and she has coached over 400+ long form improv teams (some virtually like from Bali).

She has studied under Armando Diaz, Ian Roberts, Kevin Mullaney, Michael Delaney and many others. She directed and coached UCB NY Maude Teams, Harold teams, Killgore The Musical (asst. director/art director), The Documentary UCB class (co-teacher w/ Billy Merrit). Her improv teams in NYC include Spoiled Space Monkeys, Fart Police, Chica go-go and is also at DCM every year with KROMPF and Wicked Fuckin' Queeah.

You can also hear her talk improv on Jimmy Carrane Improv Nerd Podcast taped at The Steelstacks Improv Fest 2014, Improv Resource Center podcast with Kevin Mullaney and many more.

Catherine Hodges

Catherine Hodges first started improvising in 2014, after seeing an amazing improvised opera at Hoopla and thinking, "that's very cool, I should do that." She joined Shellshock!, the Durham University improvised comedy society and hasn't looked back since.

Currently, Catherine improvises with several different groups including Stealing the Show (improvised heist movies), The Cambridge Impronauts (who does a mix of short and longform), Spawn of Sean (improvised sci-fi musicals) and a science-based short-form group. She's performed at shows and festivals across the UK, including sold-out Brighton Fringe runs, the Edinburgh Fringe, Birmingham Improv festival, Hoopla's UK & Ireland improv festival and more.

Catherine's absolute favourite thing about improv is the community, and she loves facilitating workshops with JSE Improv, and helping others find the joy in making stuff up.

Jen Kenny

Jen Kenny is utterly in love with improv. Having watched 'Whose Line Is It Anyway?', many years ago, she never would have realised that Improv would become her passion.

She is a member of Tiny Stories and appears regularly with The Same Faces. She has also performed and guested with Box of Frogs, City Improv, Off Broad Street, Acaprov among others (basically, if you ask her, she'll turn up. This also goes for any workshops going on!).

Her enthusiasm for the artform has also led her to seek out as much training as possible and she has taken courses with Jules Munns (Maydays), Armando Diaz, Will Luera, Colleen Doyle, Brian Jack and many others. Her current passion is the mashing up of improv and karaoke with her awesome partner Hannah Platts.

Her main aim in improv is to bring joy to herself and her fellow performers, but mostly to the audience.

Shaun Landry

A Native of Chicago Illinois living in Los Angeles, Shaun Landry is the Artistic Director of *Oui Be Negroes*, founded The West Coast Improv Alliance and cofounded The San Francisco Improv Festival. She is also half of the Duo of Landry & Summers and was part of the all-female African American team Essence Improv and directed the LGBTQ ensemble OUTe.

Shaun has worked for The Second City Chicago Tour Company & Children's Theater, Geese Theater Company, African American Shakespeare Company and has been in the improvisational festival circuit teaching and performing at The Kansas City, Big Stinkin Improv Austin, The Funny Women's New York, Miami, Hawaii, Duofest Philadelphia, Improv Festival, Oberlin College, Chicago, Amsterdam, Seoul and Tokyo Improv Festivals BATS Improv Comedy Festivals and has taught at universities including Stanford and Northwestern.

She can be read in the book "Whose Improv is it Anyway: Beyond the Second City." Her writing has been featured on the literary site The Redroom with Stephen Colbert, Jon Stewart, and President Barack Obama.

As a member of the SAG/AFTRA, she has appeared on *Conan*, *Transparent* and in the movies Read You Like a Book with Danny Glover and Karen Black as Marcia, and The Oscar Award winning movie *Milk* with Sean Penn as Gwenn Craig.

Milou Manie

Milou Manie has been doing improv for over 5+ years (as of the publication of this book), and has been in shows and classes in MissImp in Nottingham, UK. She also has a valuable and unique perspective since she works in online marketing and can boil down the essence of a message and how to make it appealing to an audience.

Milou has a brilliant mind for concise offers, and finds connecting with people onstage both the most challenging and rewarding part of improv.

Kate McCabe

An American, like The Dukes of Hazzard, Flavor Flav, and corndogs, Kate McCabe now resides in Manchester. She was originally trained in Improv in the sleepy university town of New York City where she performed with the all-girl long-form troupe, The Hester Prynnz. She currently plays and teaches with ComedySportz, in Manchester, especially because it follows the tradition of only performing in troupes that end with a 'z' where an 's' should be. Kate performs with Murder Inc. and teaches with Laugh at Leeds. Kate performs stand-up wherever she can get the stage time. Hobbies include: comic books, napping, snacking, karate-kicking, and ignoring responsibilities to complete various video games.

Sarah McGillion

Sarah McGillion has been regularly performing improv comedy in Copenhagen since May 2016. She has been in theatre since the age of four, training with The Young People's Theatre in Dublin, the Gaiety School of Acting, and the Irish Film Academy. Sarah has completed practical and theoretical drama examinations, as well as competing in national competitions in Ireland for acting and poetry.

More recently, Sarah has trained and performed at improv festivals across Europe (Amsterdam, Barcelona, Copenhagen, Edinburgh, Oslo, Tallinn, Tampere); North America (Los Angeles, New York, Guelph); and Australia (Melbourne, Sydney), from where she brings extensive experience, both from the various different schools of improv taught, and also the many stages on which she has performed.

Sarah is an experienced teacher and coach of improvisational theatre, having held the position of Director of Short Form at Improv Comedy Copenhagen for over two years, and worked as a teacher at the ICC training centre for over a year teaching new students and performance classes.

Sarah performs throughout Copenhagen and abroad with her comedy partner Adrian Mackinder with their show "If these walls could talk". Sarah performs short form improvisation with "Making Our Parents Proud" at 1420 in Nørrebro on Wednesdays.

Chris Mead

Chris Mead is a UK-based performer and theatre-maker who teaches and coaches improvisation in London.

He studied theatre at Royal Holloway College and improvisation at iO and The Annoyance Theatre in Chicago.

Chris is co-artistic director of The Nursery Theatre, a space in London dedicated to improv as a theatrical art form. He's a member of the internationally-renowned ensemble The Maydays, one half of sci-fi duo Project2 and recently co-founded Unmade Theatre Co. to pursue new projects as a director and performer.

Chris loves improv. It's at the heart of everything he does.

He performs it, teaches it and talks about it - both in podcasts and on his blog.

129

Jane Morris

Jane Morris is the Johnny Appleseed of comedy clubs, having opened the Chicago Comedy Showcase, the Second City ETC, Upfront Comedy, the Comedy Underground and currently managing the Fanatic Salon in Culver City. She has most recently been seen in Brooklyn Nine-Nine, Shameless, I Am the Night and will soon be seen opposite Meryl Streep in The Laundromat.

She teaches writing for performance workshop at the Fanatic Salon every Wednesday evening and performs live at the venue on a very regular basis.

Nikki Morgan

Nikki Morgan has studied Applied Theatre and Education at the Royal Central School of Speech & Drama. She is a powerhouse of improv in Nottingham and her fearless style has created joy in her teammates and the audience.

Maggie Nolan

Maggie was born in the showbiz town of Coventry where she attended youth theatre for many years and one week of tap, ballet, and modern – to which she was asked not to return.

Maggie has finally found her spiritual home in the world of improv and loves anything that involves singing, rhyming BUT NOT PUNS! (She is allergic to them).

Maggie also spends her time playing with her baby and sketch-writing about strange things she sees on daytime television.

Jennifer O'Sullivan

Jennifer O'Sullivan is an improvisor, director and creative producer living in Te-Whanganui-a-Tara (Wellington, New Zealand). She holds a MFA (Creative Practice) in Theatre from Victoria University. She is the co-founder and director of Locomotive, the director of the New Zealand Improv Festival and the creative lead for Kickin' Rad Productions, as well as a freelance administrator, designer, and teacher. In 2013 Jennifer founded Funny Birds, a group for women and non-binary individuals working in and around comedy in New Zealand, and has mentored through Cultivate Mentoring Lab and other networks. As an improv teacher she has travelled nationally and internationally, helping improvisors become fearless and work naturally on stage. As a performer she has been in countless shows (mostly improvised) with many different companies,

133

including Awkward Threesome (Tastiest Show NZ Fringe 2016) and many more. The last decade has seen her advocating for women, improv, LGBTQ*, and creative safety throughout the performance industry. In 2016 she created Late Night Knife Fight at BATS Theatre to encourage innovation and experimentation in improv forms, and to have a good time.

Also, she has a very cute dog.

Gosia Rozalska

Małgorzata Różalska (Gosia/Róża) – improviser and teacher from the north of Poland. She has been improvising since 2004, being one of the first in Poland. Besides being an improviser, she graduated in Film Directing from Gdynia Film School, Photography at Academy of Fine Arts in Gdańsk, and Cultural Studies at University of Gdańsk – and she loves mixing all her arts with improv. She acts with her own company, and she also writes in a blog of her own creation - www.rozalska.com.

She is part of an international improv group called OHANA, and she can be found conquering the world, teaching and performing at Seattle International Festival of Improv, Improvention in Canberra, IMPRO Amsterdam, IMPRO Berlin, Mt. Olymprov in Athens, Big IF in Barcelona, Sacrebleu! in Strasbourg, Sofia International Improv Fest, WIP Workimprogress, Improfestival Mainz. She's a big nerd, and she'll never stop learning.

135

Becky Webb

(Photography by John Nichols)

Becky Webb is a trained clown and physical theatre performer. Upon graduation from Circomedia in Bristol she formed the theatre company Jilted Pig alongside becoming part of the improv group The Hot Air Baboons as well as performing street theatre nationwide.

Returning to Liverpool she started working with the improv company Impropriety, performing with them for a number of years including their annual Improvathon.

She subsequently travelled to Canada to perform as part of Die-Nasty's annual soapathon in Edmonton.

136

She is currently a part of Casino Improv who perform twice monthly at The Old Courts Arts Centre in Wigan.

She loves improvisation for its ability to be able to create shared experiences and to create a direct connection with the audience be it in a theatre, on the street or one to one.

She also hates learning lines.

Louise Woods

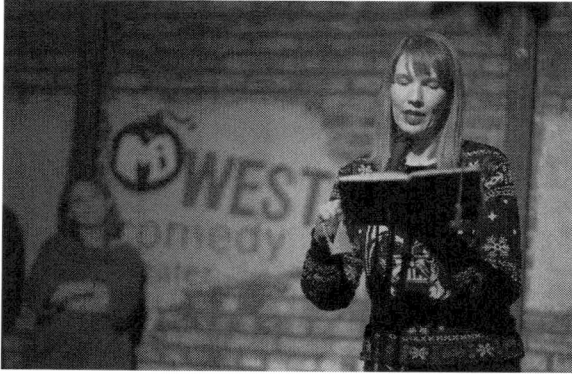

Louise Woods is fantastic.

Thank you to
everyone within the improv community for being open to try
new things and for welcoming new people into the
ever growing community of improv.

Printed in Poland
by Amazon Fulfillment
Poland Sp. z o.o., Wrocław

61324341R00089